THIS NOTEBOOK BELONGS TO

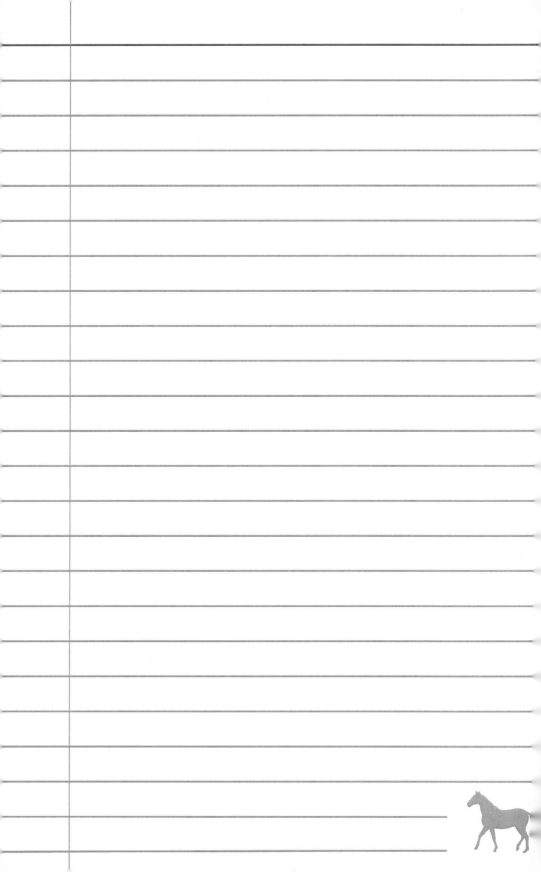

And now, the end is near, as you've just faced,
the final page turn...

Fear not, be not afraid...

More of what you love is just one scan away!

Designs of
note!® available at amazon

Made in United States
North Haven, CT
15 June 2025

69829865R00057